Should Children Have Homework?

by Ms. Soll's class
with Tony Stead

capstone®
classroom

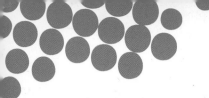

Why do we need to do homework? Wouldn't it be better to go outside and play or relax? In this book, we give arguments for and against homework. So which should it be: homework or no homework? Read this book to help you decide.

I Don't Want Homework!

by Ambria

I think homework is a waste of time, and here's why.

I think kids should not have homework because we need time to rest. We need to relax our brains and ourselves!

Another reason why I think kids should not have homework is because we need to have time to do fun activities. We would not have time to play a sport or do dance if we had homework.

I also think kids need time to interact and play with other kids and friends. Homework takes away from this time.

We shouldn't have homework because we need to learn in ways other than just writing on paper. Homework takes away from this time.

5

Yes, Kids Should Be Given Homework

by Maya

There are many reasons why we should have homework. For example, practice makes perfect. Homework is practice. The more you practice homework, the smarter you will become. Practicing homework can make you very smart.

Homework could be fun. If you don't have any after-school activities, you could do homework instead. If you do have after-school activities, you could do homework during a break.

When you bring homework home, your parents love to see what you are learning in class. Your parents could also help you learn something that your teacher did not teach you yet. And your parents could help you if you were having trouble in class. Your parents are very interested in what you are learning at school.

Your homework can help your teacher see if you need help. When your teacher sees your homework, she knows if you were listening in class. Your teacher could also help you with your homework if you were having trouble!

Your homework could give you a little challenge. You get to reflect on what you learned in school that day. And your homework could teach you something that your teacher did not tell you yet. Homework could be challenging, but it is a lot of fun!

The best thing about homework is that you learn a lot. This is why I think we should have homework!

No Homework

by Eliana

I am going to explain why kids should not have homework. I think homework is terrible for kids.

Kids should not have homework because we have so much work in school, and by the time we get home from school we feel tired. The parents say, "Time for homework!" but we don't want to do it.

Some kids like homework, and some kids do not. If you asked me for my opinion, I would say I do not like homework because it takes away from other activities after school like soccer or other sports.

Not only that but homework is B-O-R-I-N-G, and it can also be hard. I'm frustrated when I don't know the answer.

Some homework can be fun, some homework can be long, some homework can be easy. But let's face it, when you get fun homework, then you're a lucky duck!

Homework takes time away from kids. These are the reasons why kids should not have homework.

Homework Bazaar!

by Reda

I think kids should have homework for many reasons.

One reason is that if we don't do our homework, we don't understand the lesson our teacher teaches, and we get stumped. Then we have to ask for help from our parents.

Another reason that kids should have homework is because if we have homework every day, then we get to go to college. Then we will get a good job in the future.

I think kids should have homework because it helps us become successful later in life. Homework helps kids be smart at school and smart everywhere!

Boo! Homework!

by Kevyn

I think we should not have homework. Homework is terrible and bad.

One reason why is because kids should be able to relax when they come home. We need more free time when we get home.

We should just extend school so we can do the homework in class. That way, we don't have to do homework at home, and we get to spend time with family. We would also have time to watch a movie with our family if we didn't have to worry about homework.

I also do not think children should have homework because they can get frustrated. This happens when we cannot find the answer.

These are some of the reasons for not having homework.

Homework Educates

by Caroline

I think that we should have homework because it makes us smarter.

My first reason is because it exercises our brains. Our brains are like muscles, and if we exercise them more, we become smarter.

My second reason is that if we exercise our brains, we will get a better job and sometimes go to a better college. If we don't get smarter, we won't go to a good college or get a good job.

I think we should have homework, but not due the next day. The teacher should have all homework due on Fridays.

That is why I think we should have homework. But don't make it due the next day because we need to enjoy our free time.

10:30, Still Doing Homework!

by Sophie

I think that kids should not have homework! I believe this because many nights I have so much homework that I have to stay up late and finish it all. Then, in the morning, I'm so tired that I can't focus in class.

Us kids spend so much time in school learning, so when we get home, we should be able to just take a break and relax. Instead, once we come home from school, we have to go right to our homework! The homework takes so long to finish that by the time we are done, it's time to go to sleep, and we end up having no time to relax!

Therefore, if teachers want us to get good grades and focus in class, they should give us less homework. This way, we can go to bed at a normal time and have time to relax.

We Should Have Homework

by Mia

We should have homework, and there are many reasons why. Just by doing homework, we will have a better life.

If we do our homework, we will get more knowledge and if we get more knowledge, we will get into a better college. If we go to a better college, then we can get a better job. This helps us make more money so that we can be able to buy a better home. So as you can see, doing homework will help us have better things and live a better life.

Homework leads to a better life. If we have a better life, we will be happier.

We Do Enough at School

by Madison

I think we shouldn't have homework.

We do enough at school. I think we should have a period at school to do it and not do it at home. When we get home, we can then play around all day and not do homework.

Another reason why we shouldn't have homework is because it takes away from activities. When we come home, we want to go out and play and not sit and do homework.

My final reason why we shouldn't have homework is because we just need to relax at home instead of doing homework. Our bodies need to relax once we get home from a big day at school.

And that is why I think we shouldn't have homework!

I Want Homework

by Emily

I think kids should have homework.

Children need their education. They need to prove that they are responsible for what they know. Homework helps prove this.

They also need to participate in class so teachers can see if they need help in school. If they need help, they could join a school club that helps them with their homework.

Finally, kids need to do homework to go to a good college and have a good future.

So my whole point is that kids need to do homework.

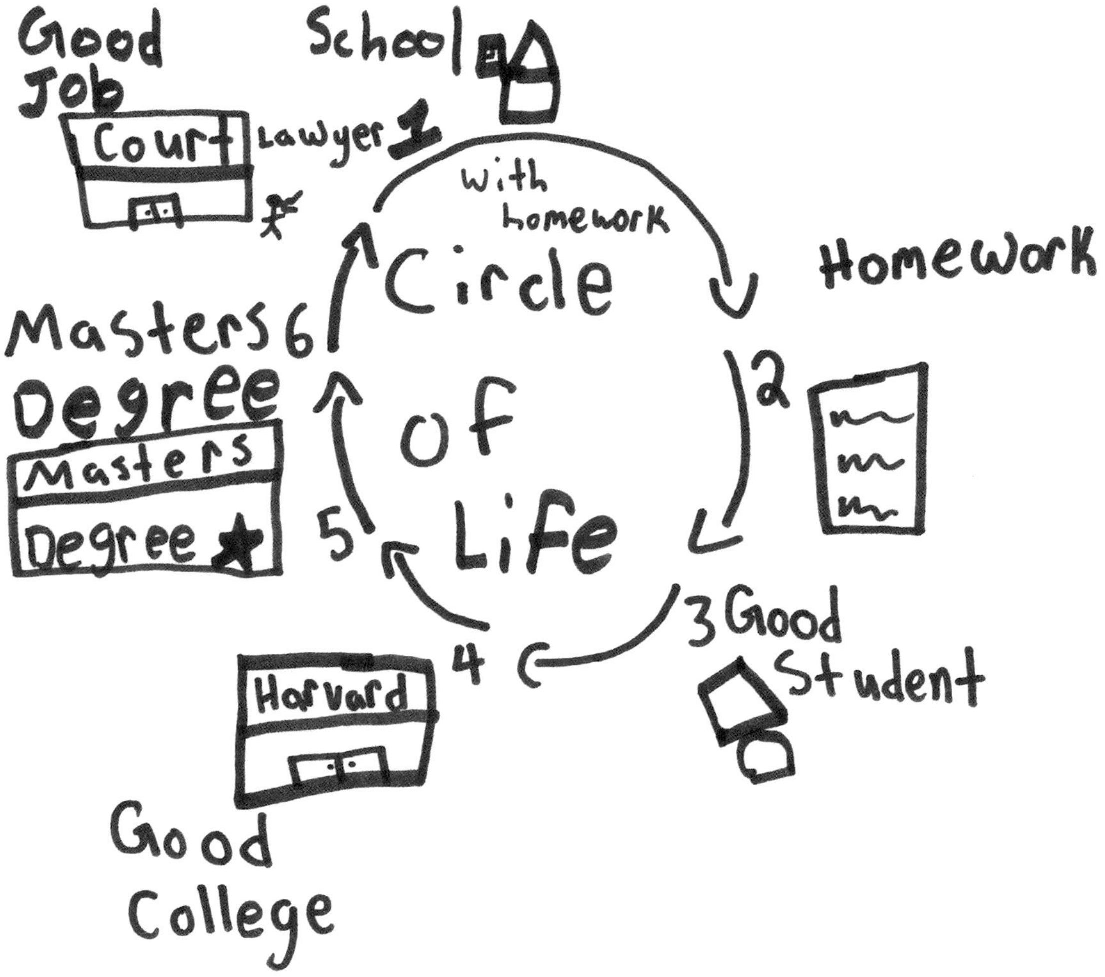

Good Job

Court

School

Lawyer 1

with homework

Circle

Homework

of

2

Masters 6
Degree

Masters
Degree ★

Life

5

4

3 Good
Student

Harvard

Good
College

As we argue, homework can take up your free time, but it can also help you become smarter and lead you to better choices in life. If you had to decide between doing homework or playing games and relaxing with friends after school, which would you choose? Why would you make that choice?

or